This is my book:
_____

© 2024 glendalee. All rights reserved.

No part of this book may be reproduced, stored in a retrieval system, or transmitted by any means without the written permission of the author.

AuthorHouse™
1663 Liberty Drive
Bloomington, IN 47403
www.authorhouse.com
Phone: 833-262-8899

Because of the dynamic nature of the Internet, any web addresses or links contained in this book may have changed since publication and may no longer be valid. The views expressed in this work are solely those of the author and do not necessarily reflect the views of the publisher, and the publisher hereby disclaims any responsibility for them.

This book is printed on acid-free paper.

ISBN: 979-8-8230-2809-7 (sc)
ISBN: 979-8-8230-2810-3 (e)

Library of Congress Control Number: 2024911509

Print information available on the last page.

Published by AuthorHouse   06/15/2024

authorHOUSE

I Am Love

by glendalee

2

This book is dedicated to:

All the children in the world,

Thank you for being you.

Enjoy all the illustrations.

Are you one of these children? Can you understand how they are feeling? What are these children thinking? (Can you tell by seeing the expressions on their faces or mouths?)

This book will make you smile. Read these affirmations again and again. Become the best person you can be. Read this story again, and again, then many more times.

You've always had the power. You just have to learn it for yourself.

Love in my heart for you.

glendalee

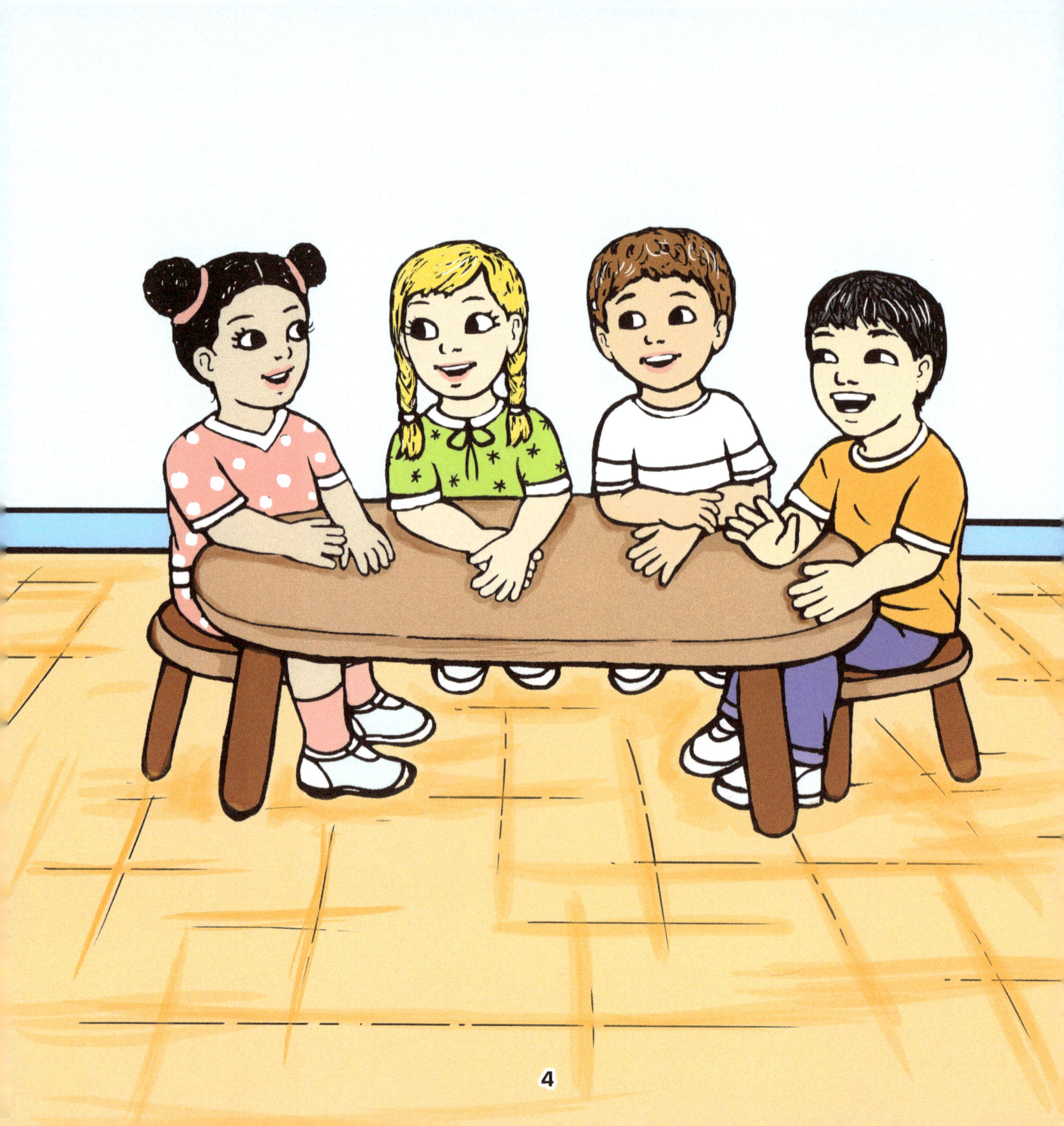

I AM all things love. *I AM* appreciative of all things good. *I AM* authentic.

THANK YOU

I AM grateful. *I AM* joy. *I AM* fearless. *I AM* vulnerable. *I AM* thankful. I say, 'T H A N K Y O U'.

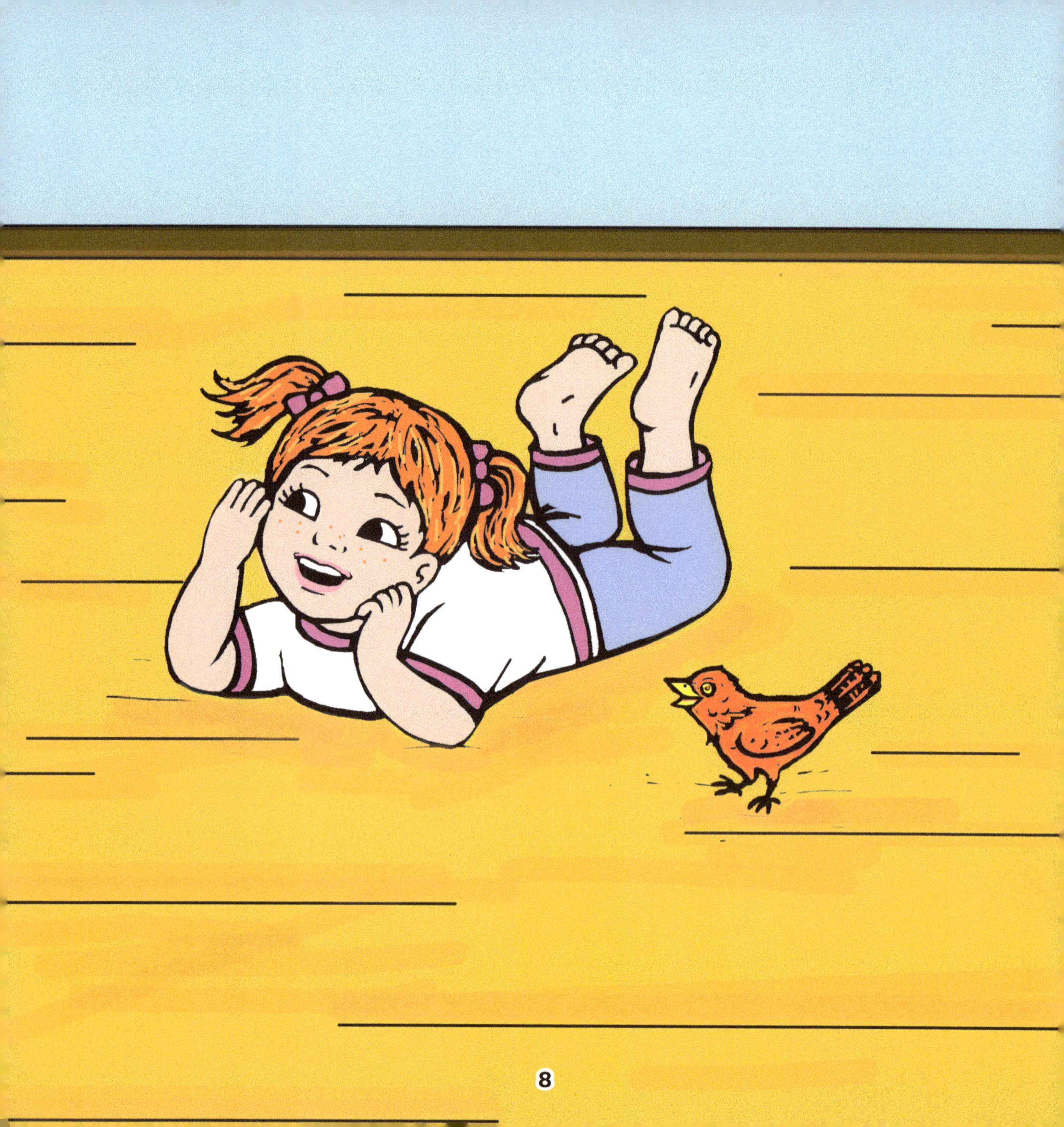

I love me. *I AM* the best I can be.

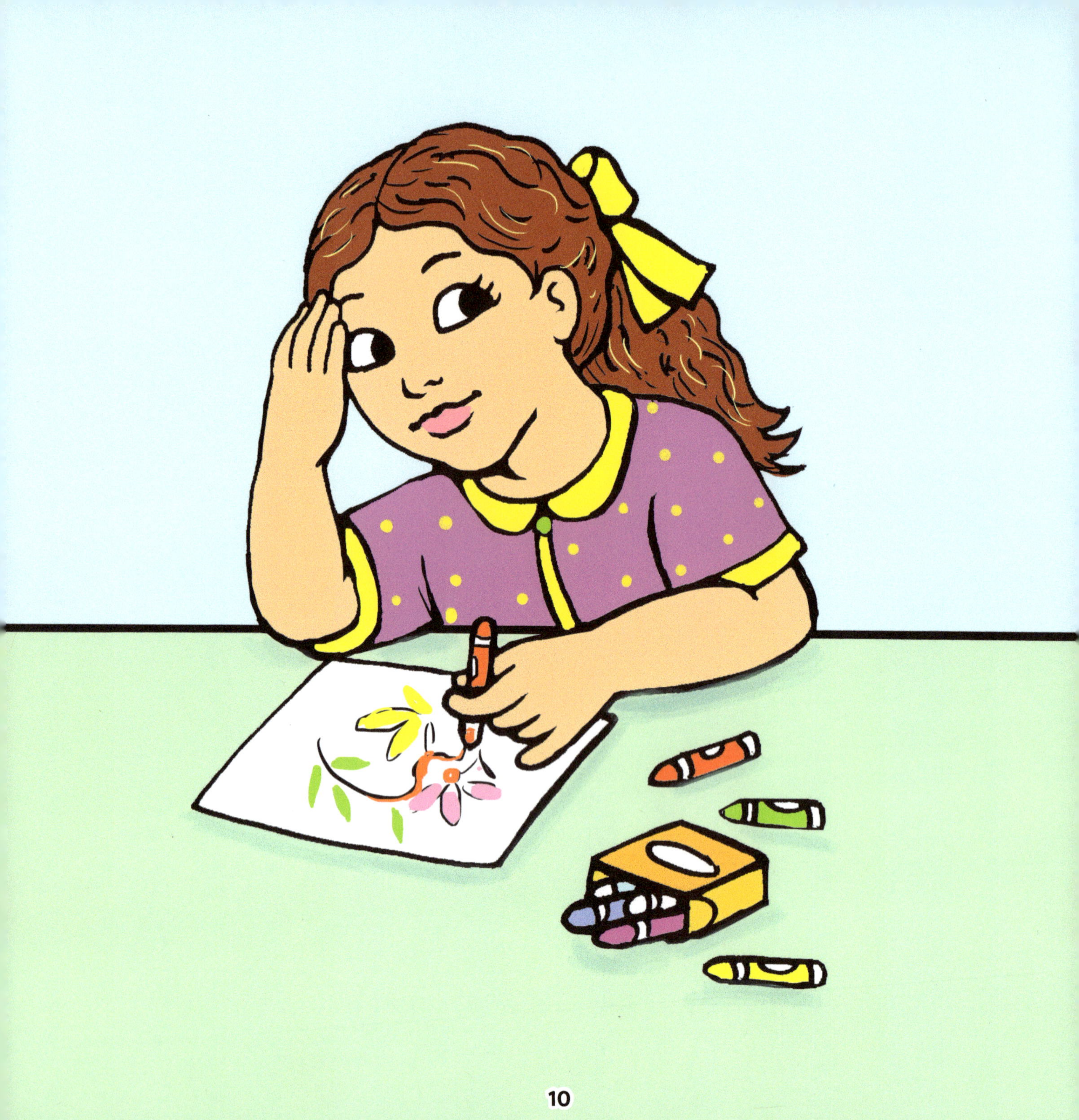

I AM courageous. *I AM* created for a purpose. I love myself.

12

I love you. *I AM* a heart, full of love. *I AM* all smiles.
I AM 'shine' from inside out. *I AM LOVE*.

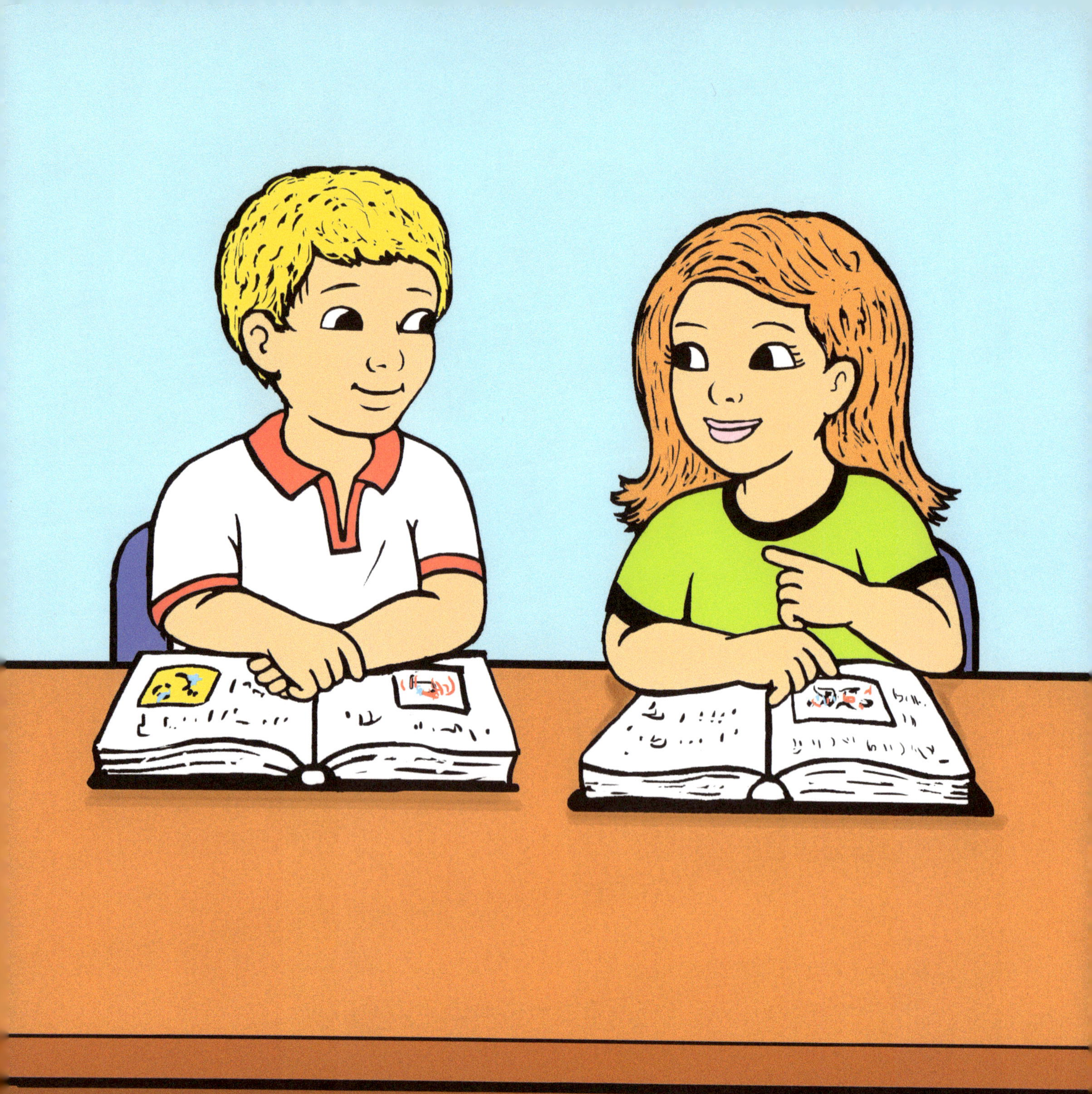

I AM LOVE for others. *I AM* worthy of love.

16

I AM full speed ahead. *I AM* full of energy.
Energy is my fuel. I live my life to it's fullest.

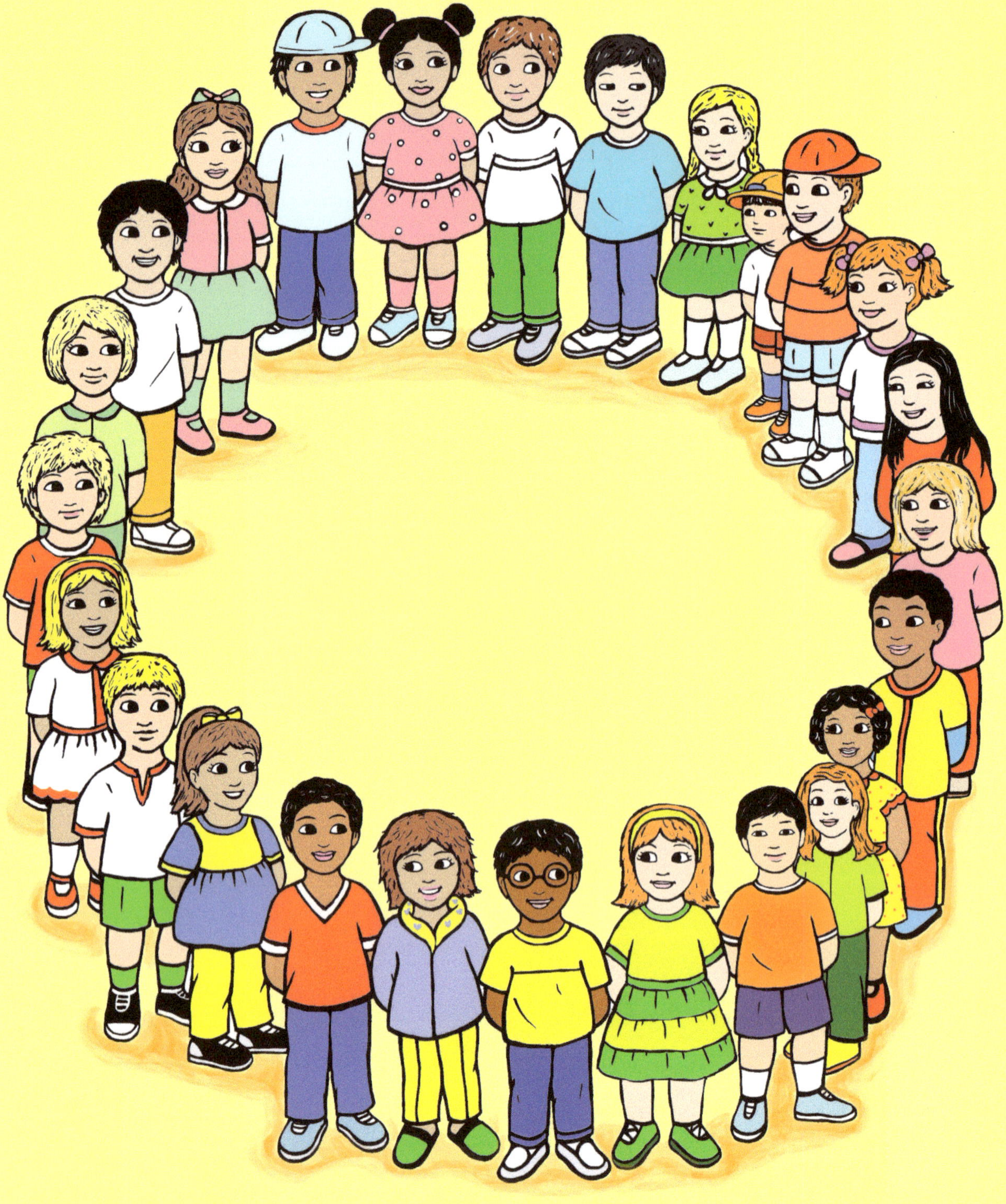

I AM LOVE. I AM showing my smile. *I AM* sharing my smile with everyone I see. We are love, all of us together.

20

I AM helpful with others. *I AM* glowing inside.

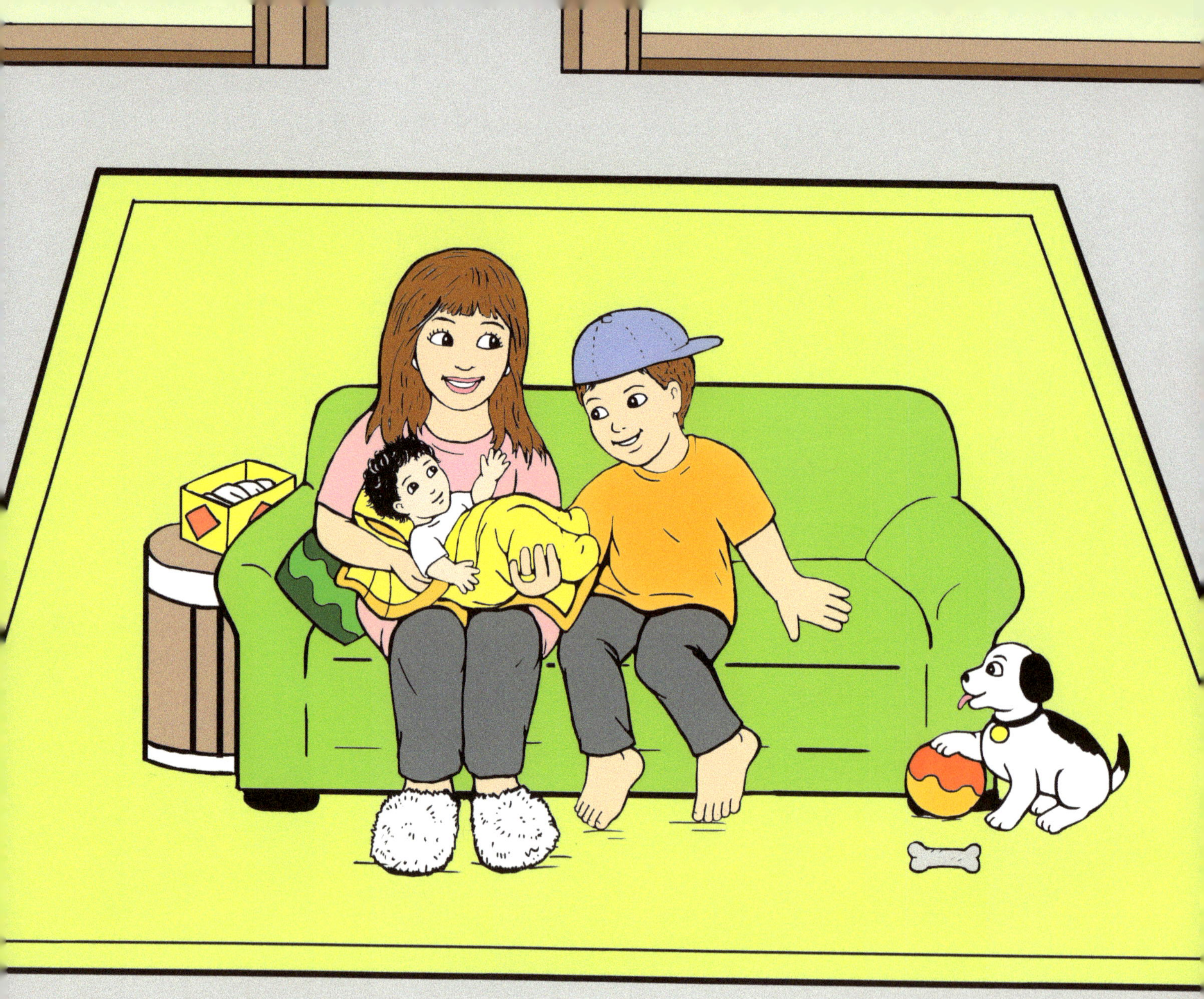

I AM aware how I can help others everyday. *I AM* giving to others. *I AM* receiving rewards of love by giving.

24

I AM LOVE. I AM joy in my heart. People feel what I feel inside. *I AM* a presence. *I AM* a blessing to others. People call me "Sunshine".

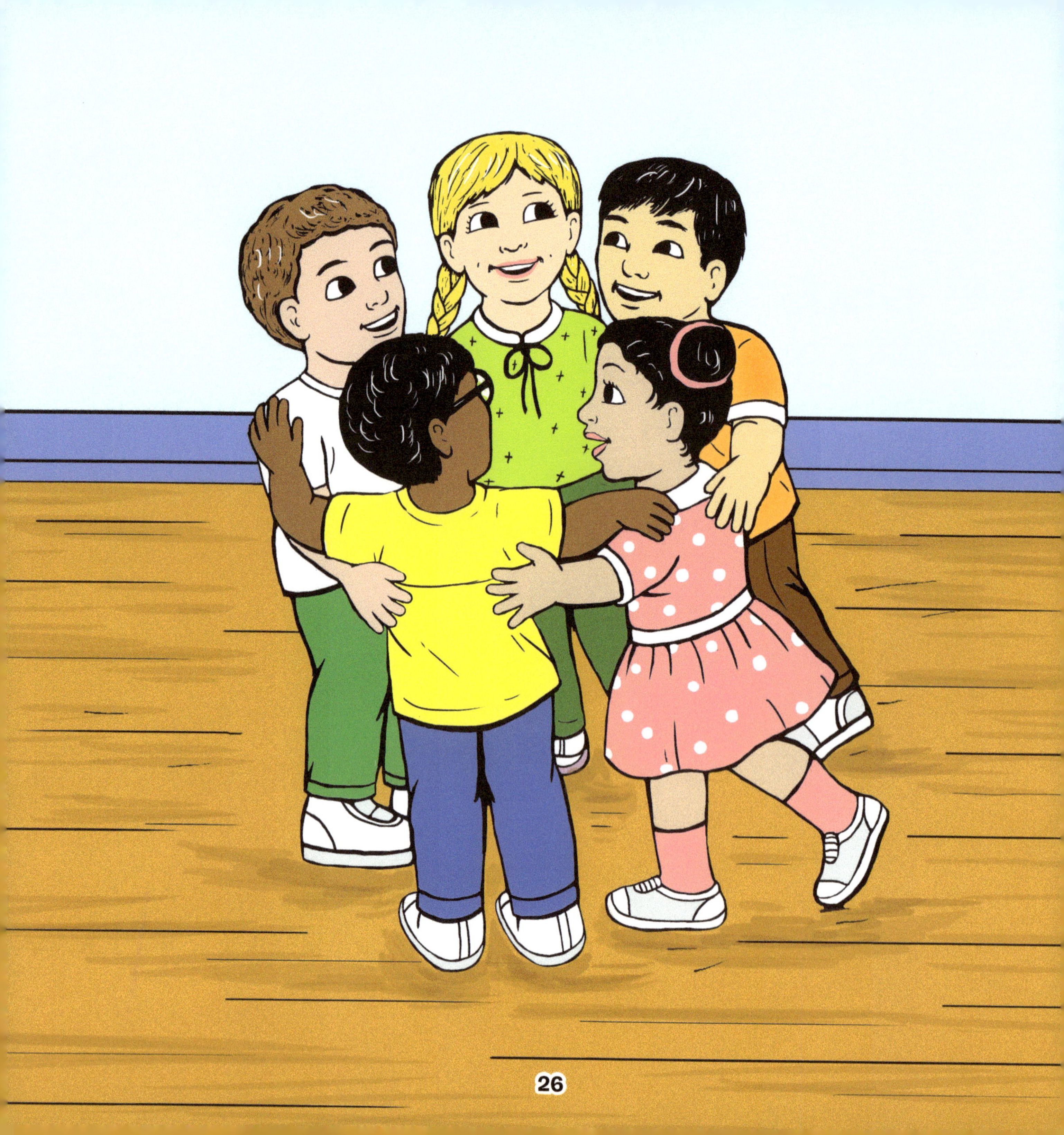

I AM worthy of love. *I AM* joy every minute.
I AM aware of how I feel every minute.

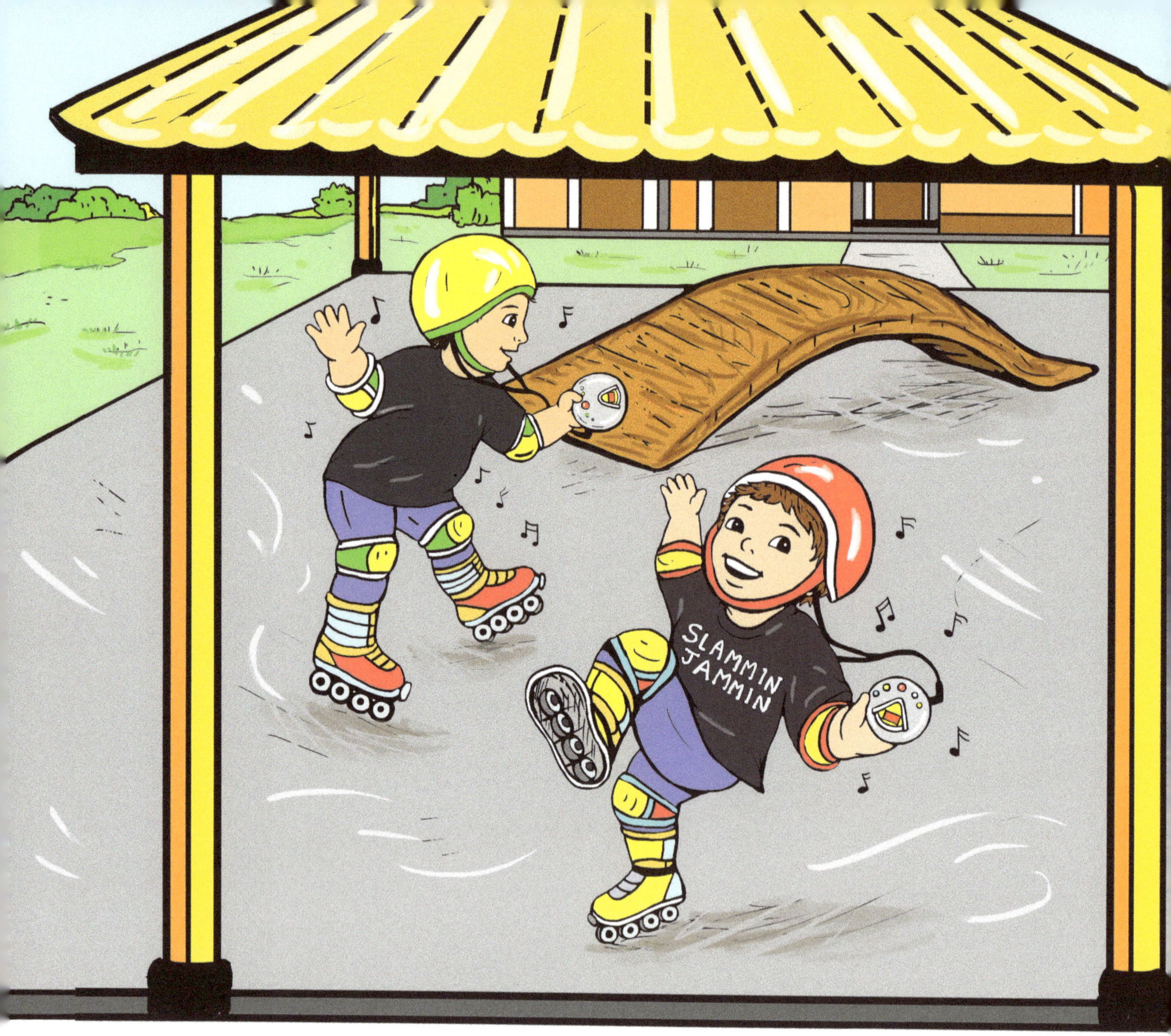
SLAMMIN
JAMMIN

I AM enough every minute. *I AM* learning something new everyday.

30

I AM always doing the best I can. *I AM* learning. *I AM* my dreams. *I AM* a manifestor for living my dreams.

32

I AM appreciative of all I have. *I AM* honest with everyone I communicate with. *I AM LOVE*.

Image 16

34

I AM honest. *I AM* appreciative of all things around me. *I AM* happiness in my heart. *I AM* able to communicate easily. *I AM* able to live my dreams. *I AM* able to believe. *I AM* able to rest. *I AM LOVE*.

Have Fun picking a different key every day!

36

I AM deserving to live all of my dreams. *I AM* born to share my gifts. *I AM* sharing my passions with everyone.

38

I AM aware that my passions are my personal abilities.
I AM excited about my passionate gifts inside my heart.
I AM able to share my gifts with others. *I AM* aware
of the great things that happen to me every day.

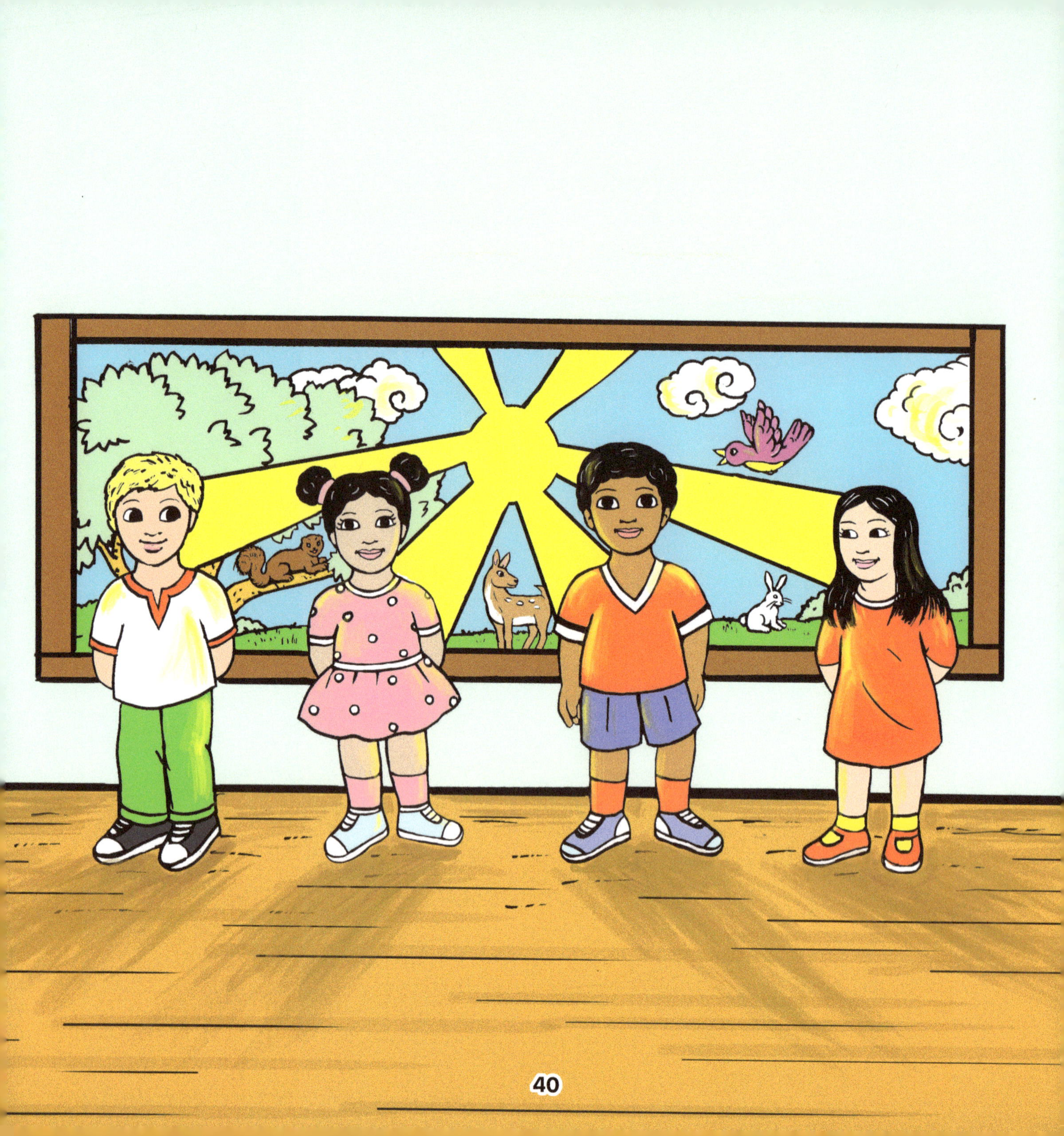

I AM able to believe in myself. *I AM* enough. *I AM* always shining. *SHINE. SHINE. SHINE. SHINE.*

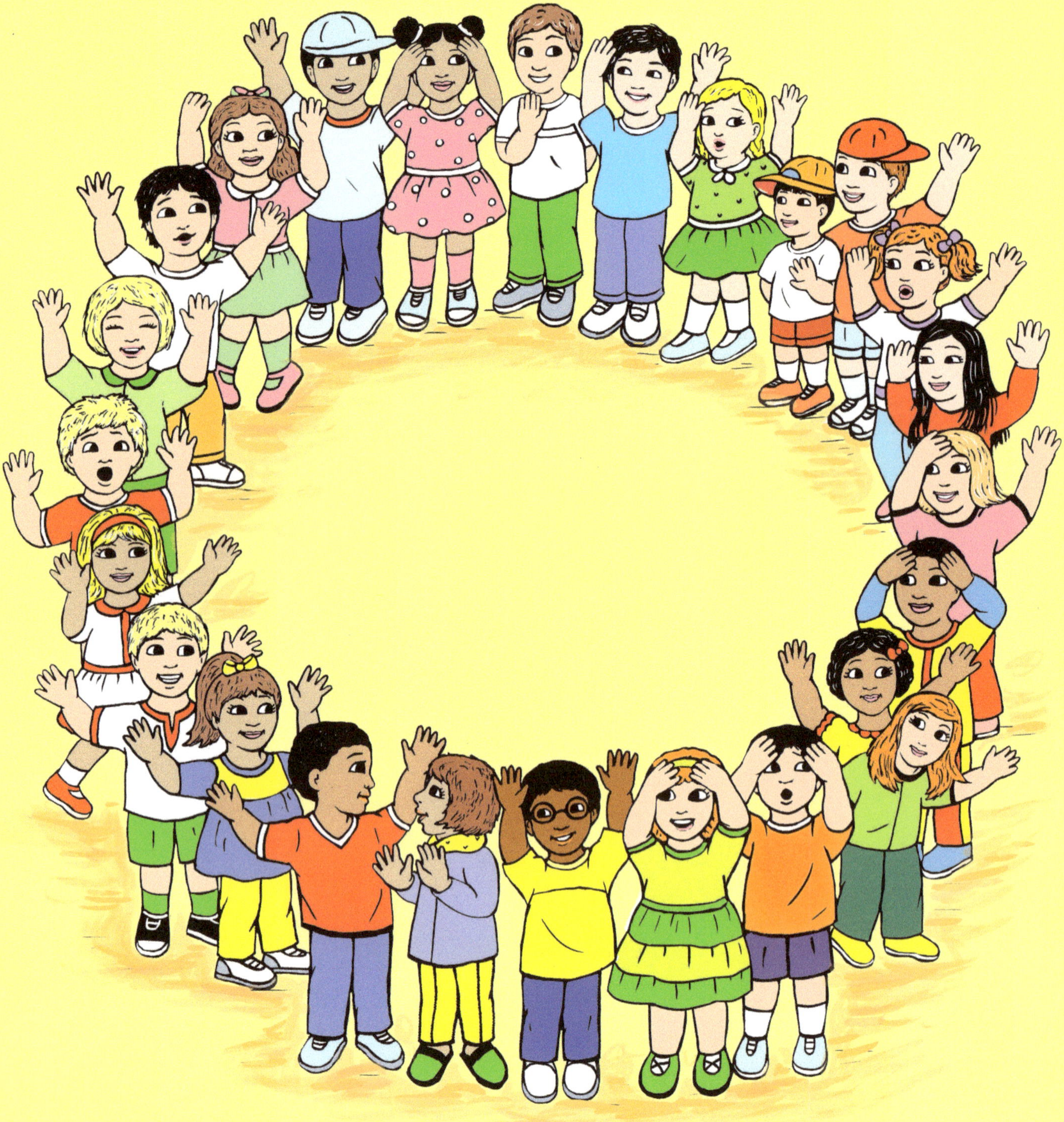

I AM aware of how I feel inside every minute. *I AM* able to laugh with everyone. *I AM* feeling love every minute.

44

I AM living in the moment. *I AM* feeling joy. *I AM* aware joy is a choice. *I AM* choosing joy. *I AM* energy. *I AM* gratitude. *I AM* attitude. *I AM* joy. *I AM LOVE*.

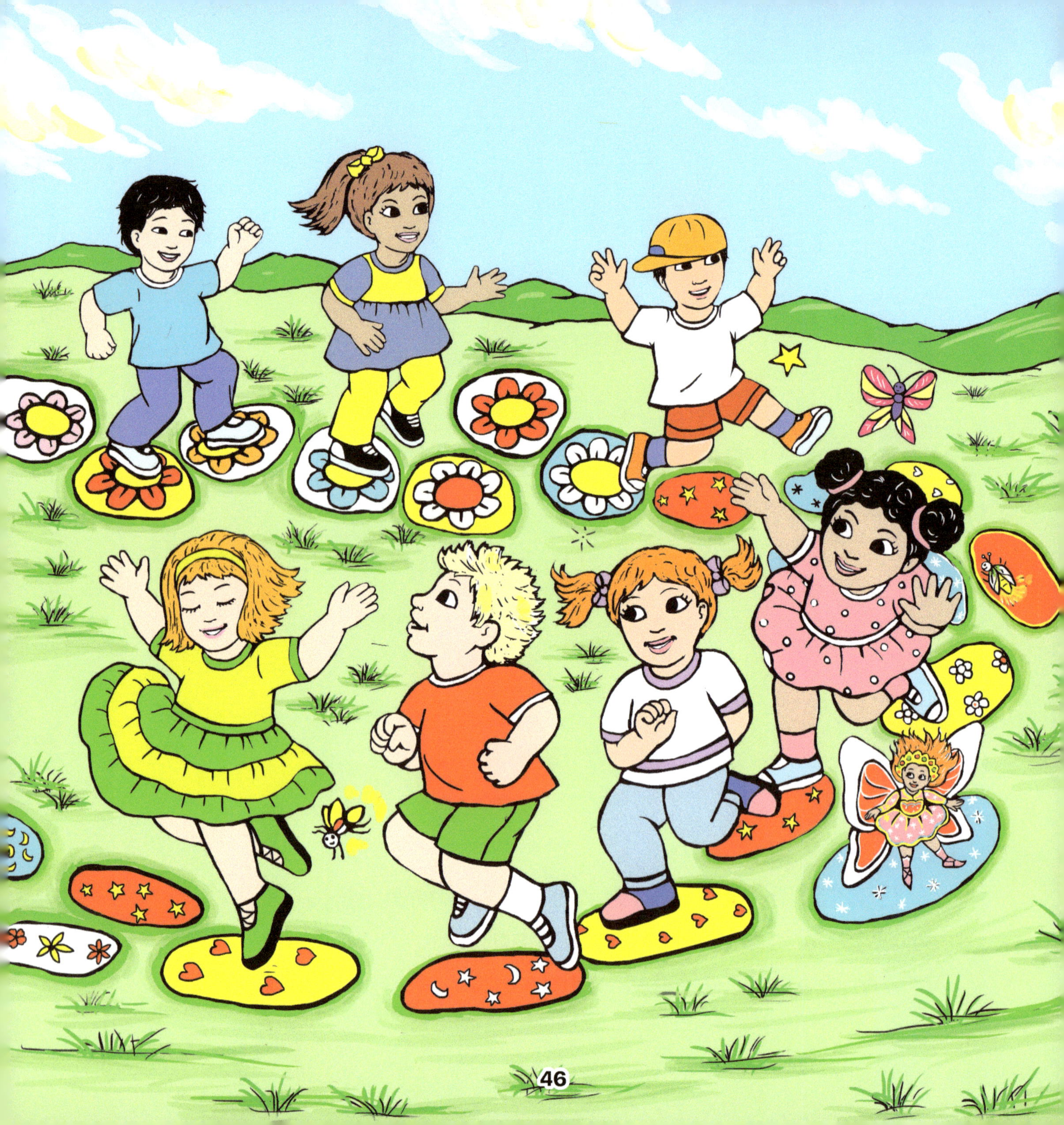

I AM capable. *I AM* all I can be. *I AM* my gifts in my heart. *I AM* who *I AM* inside. *I AM LOVE*. *I AM* always sunshine, shining out from within me.

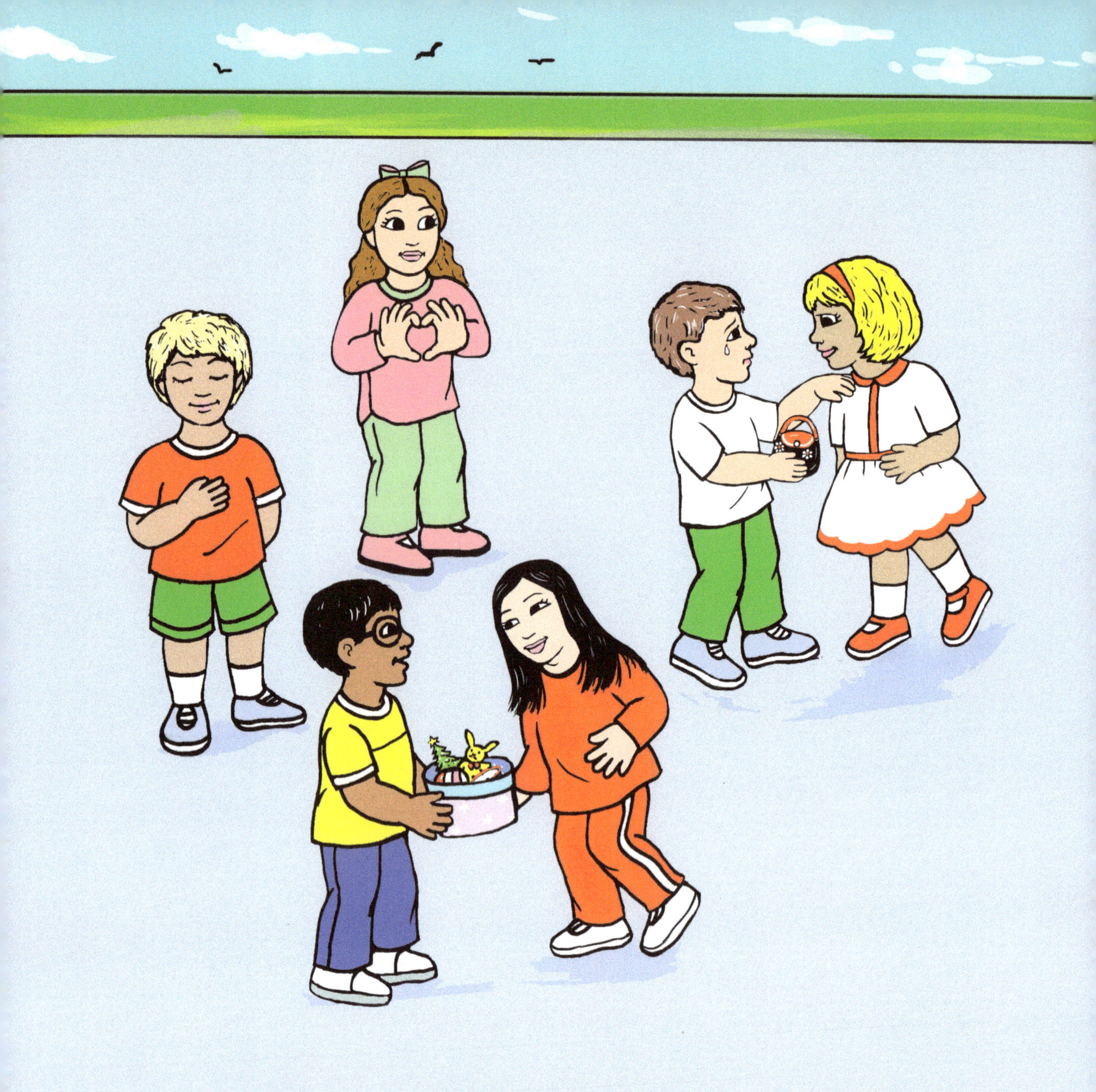

I AM truth. *I AM* all things true. *I AM* honest. *I AM* fair with everyone.

50

I AM LOVE. I AM a blessing to everyone I see each day, and to everyone around the world. *I AM* sleeping happily in my quiet place, so I rest. *I AM* sending love and blessings to all around me, and all around the world.

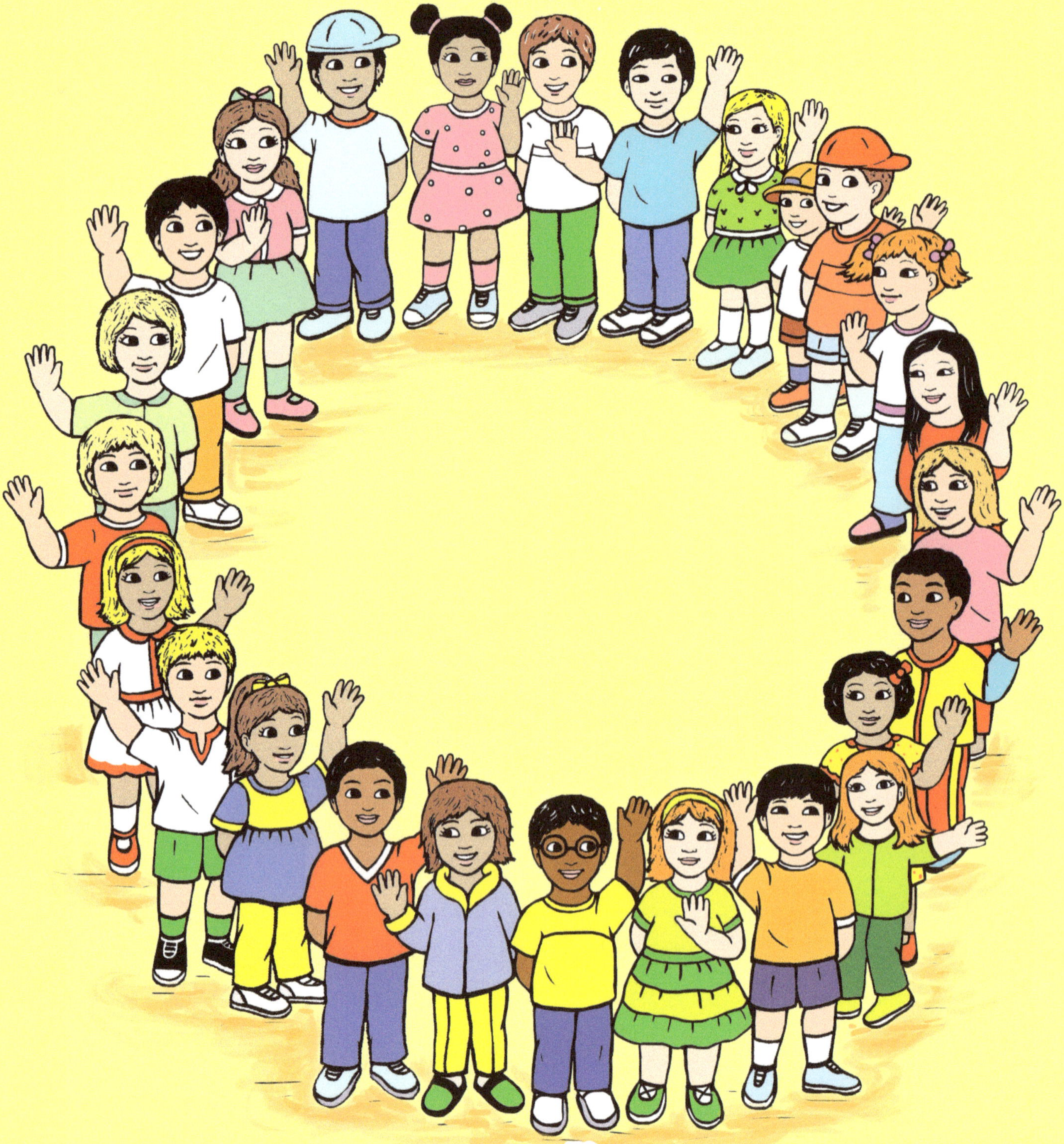

Sweet dreams. Thankful hearts. See ya next time!
I LOVE ME! And I LOVE YOU, TOO!!

Milton Keynes UK
Ingram Content Group UK Ltd.
UKHW050956070724
445092UK00004B/15

9 798823 028097